BEADS plus MACRAMÉ

Applying Knotting Techniques to Beadcraft

LITTLE CRAFT BOOK SERIES

by grethe la croix

STERLING PUBLISHING CO., INC.   NEW YORK

SAUNDERS OF TORONTO, Ltd., Don Mills, Canada

Oak Tree Press Co., Ltd.
London & Sydney

Little Craft Book Series

Translated by Eric Greweldinger   Adapted by Jane Lassner

The original edition was published in the Netherlands under the title "Draad en Kralen," © 1969 by Cantecleer De Bilt, De Bilt, Netherlands.

Seventh Printing, 1977

Copyright © 1971 by Sterling Publishing Co., Inc. 419 Park Avenue South, New York, N.Y. 10016

Distributed in Australia and New Zealand by Oak Tree Press Co., Ltd.,
P.O. Box J34, Brickfield Hill, Sydney 2000, N.S.W.
Distributed in the United Kingdom and elsewhere in the British Commonwealth
by Ward Lock Ltd., 116 Baker Street, London W 1
Manufactured in the United States of America   *All rights reserved*
Library of Congress Catalog Card No.: 78-151710
Sterling ISBN 0-8069-5168-0 Trade   Oak Tree 7061-2299-2
5169-9 Library

Contents

Before You Begin

Threading beads for necklaces, belts and other accessories is a popular craft, but did you ever think of incorporating the thread itself into the design? If the beads are going to be attached to a piece of cloth, you can embroider the thread around the beads to enhance their color and sparkle, at the same time as you secure them to the fabric. If the beads are going to be threaded without a cloth backing, so they stand on their own as in a belt or necklace, you can knot and loop the thread around the beads with macramé knots. All sorts of delightful patterns, seemingly intricate yet really based on only a few simple stitches and knots, result as you experiment with the beads and string.

While this book offers suggestions for patterns and objects to make from these patterns, an ornament which you design yourself either on purpose or by accident is just as correct as one which you may read of. Macramé and beadcraft, though they seem unrelated, have one very important thing in common: almost any design made with them is attractive. Of course, some are more attractive than others, but you should not feel that the ideas you read about here are necessarily the best ones there are. Practice on these if you are a beginner, but then let your own imagination be your inspiration for other designs. The best part of decorating with beads and macramé knots is that you do not need any special equipment other than the beads and string. An occasional project may require something else—a covered bottle naturally needs a bottle to be covered—but in general, you need no more materials than the obvious ones. If you are embroidering with the beads, you will need a few other things: embroidery floss (a thread with a special sheen, available at needlecraft counters), fabric to embroider on, and an embroidery needle. The eye of the needle must be large enough for the floss, but small enough to go through the holes in the beads you are using. Naturally, you need a scissors to cut the thread. (Do not break the thread with your teeth: this weakens the thread, to say nothing of your teeth, and may cause the thread to unravel.)

For beaded objects joined with macramé knots, use any cord, string or twine as long as it is not elastic or too soft. Do not use very fine threads in macramé, even for delicate pieces: the thread does not show up as much as it should, and the intricate knotting is hidden by the beads.

The project on page 6 needs only beads of assorted shapes, sizes and colors, clear glue, and a cloth or paper background. A collage of beads is the simplest project, but it can give you hours of pleasure as you watch your picture take shape piece by piece like a jigsaw puzzle. Make this your first project, to become acquainted with the different effects the beads produce when they are glued at different angles.

Bead Collage

The girl in the picture below is engrossed in glueing beads to paper on which she has lightly drawn her design. Let your lines outline large areas, so that the beads can easily fill in the sections without too much crowding, and so that the colors can be clearly seen. Even if you have no artistic talent, a bead collage is easy to design. The most elementary picture seems ornate when

Illus. 1. Making a bead collage is fun yet easy to do. To get a drop of glue on a bead, hold the bead with a pair of tweezers and touch it to the tip of a tube of glue.

5

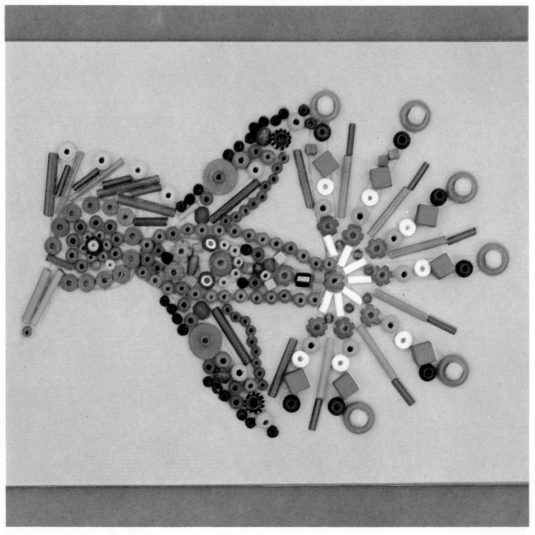

Illus. 2. This colorful bird looks so lively that he seems about to fly off the page. All the beads are attached with glue to the paper background.

you fill in the shapes with colored beads. See the bead collage in color on page 6 for visual proof.

Just as the areas to be filled in should be large, so should the beads themselves. You are making this collage for pleasure, but attaching tiny beads would turn this pleasure into tedious work. Flat or round beads, thin or oval, wooden or plastic, with notched edges or smooth—use any shape bead. If it is correctly placed it will be attractive. Experiment with the different shapes: glue some beads flat on the paper and others on their sides; layer beads of different colors to achieve a three-dimensional effect; combine different shapes and sizes anyplace on the paper. Plan the design before you begin, but do not feel bound by your plan. Experimenting as you glue makes a more random, and sometimes more attractive, composition.

The glue you use must dry clear—that is, with no color at all—so that the colors of the background and beads show. Pick the bead up with a pair of tweezers and touch it to the tip of the glue container so there is a drop of glue on the bead. Be careful not to get too much glue, or it will smear when you place the bead on the paper or cloth. Nudge the bead with your tweezers into exactly the proper position on the background, and then leave it alone to dry. Later you can hang your collage as a colorful accent in a room.

For a change in gift wrappings, print the name of the receiver of the gift on the package with letters made of beads. Christmas packages can especially benefit from this additional color: add a red Santa Claus or a white snow scene for an extra touch of holiday spirit.

Pendant with Glued Beads

If you want to make a piece of jewelry using the glueing method, try the attractive pendant shown here. Trim a piece of wood until it is perfectly round, or have a carpenter do this for you. Mark the wood with a pencil according to

Illus. 3. Make a pendant by glueing beads to a wooden circle.

7

the design and colors with which you want to cover the wood. Using your tweezers to pick up the individual beads, place a drop of glue on each bead and then lay it on the wood. Glue the beads in the middle first.

While the glue under the beads is drying, thread a string with beads slightly larger than the others, to fit around the circle. Glue this string of beads to the edge of the wood.

The pendant needs to hang from a cord if you want to wear it around your neck. Decide upon the length of cord you want, and then insert one end of this cord through several of the beads along the outer edge of the pendant. Slip beads of different colors on the ends of the cord. When you have placed as many beads as you want on these cords, tie the ends to a store-bought clasp. If the beaded cord is long enough to slip over your head without unfastening, you can eliminate the clasp and tie the ends to each other.

Illus. 4. A semi-circle of cork is easy to decorate with beads: just use pins to attach them. Glue the cork to the lid of a box for a handsome decoration.

Decorated Lids

Beads Pinned to Cork

A plain round box is so easy to decorate that you will have to force yourself *not* to, after you read these instructions. Glue a hemisphere of cork to the lid of a box, centering it exactly. Gather a variety of beads—any size, color, and shape. With long pins, sold in hobby shops, pin the beads to the cork. If your pins are long enough, you should be able to layer the beads and still have the pin go into the cord securely. The heads of the pins add to the sparkle of the decoration.

The Matting Technique

A solid area of beads can be made by weaving, as on page 37, or by the matting technique, explained here. The thread winds in and out of the beads, going through some beads twice as you fasten the rows. More secure than other ways of threading, the matting technique guarantees even rows and closely fastened beads. You can use this threading process to make either flat objects (see page 12) or three-dimensional ones.

Any lid from a glass jar, wine bottle or a round box can be decorated with this technique. To copy the design on the lid in Illus. 5, first string several beads on a thread. There are 11 beads on the circle of the lid here, but the exact number depends on both the size of your beads and the size of your lid. Tie a knot with the ends of the string, making one end very long. Insert this end through a large bead, which you will glue to the exact center of the lid, and then through the

Illus. 5. More intricate than pinning beads to cork, the matting technique is also a sturdier method of covering objects with beads. Turn the page for the diagram of this beaded lid.

9

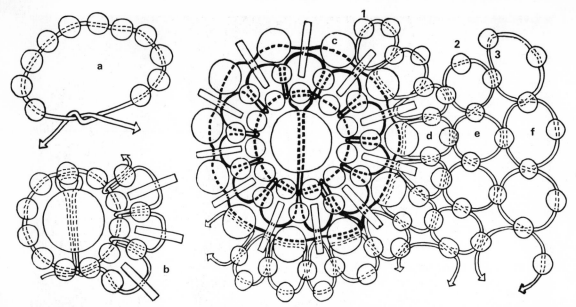

Illus. 6. Begin covering the lid with a circle of beads, as in a. Then wind another circle around the first (see b), and continue adding more rows until the lid is as wide as necessary (d, e and f).

bead on the string opposite the knot you just made. Return the string through the large bead and through one of the beads next to the knot. Glue and clip the other end of the string; you do not need it for threading if the working thread is long enough.

Make a second circle of beads with the same string by threading a spherical bead, then a thin round one, then another spherical one. Wind the thread around the piece of thread just above it, between two beads, and draw the end through the last bead you placed on the string. Continue around the circle until you return to the starting point.

If this flat circle does not completely cover the

top of the lid, add another circle of beads, threading them as diagrammed in Illus. 6c. Add still another row if necessary. Glue this piece to the top of the lid, and you are ready to begin the matting technique.

End the thread which you used for the top of the lid by glueing it back into a bead, and start a new thread at the bead labelled 1. Wind the threads through the beads as shown in Illus. 6d, pulling as tightly or as loosely as required to fit the rim of the lid. Make as many rows as the lid needs to cover it completely, ending each row by glueing the thread in the hole of a nearby bead. No special finishing is necessary after you thread the last row.

10

Illus. 7. This artistic design is the top of a leather box, ornamented with beads of varying sizes and colors. Embroidery plus beads is not difficult, but to reproduce this decoration exactly, follow the diagram on page 28.

11

Threaded Hexagonal Designs

Beaded Mats

A beaded mat can add a light, cheerful appearance to your table. Make a set of six or eight to use as individual place mats, or else make just one to use as a centerpiece. Your table will be protected from heat and scratches at the same time that it is enhanced by your beadwork.

Use oval wood beads and strong nylon or plastic cord. Begin your threading as diagrammed in Illus. 8a, making a triangle with three beads. Use both ends of the cord to thread more beads. When you complete the first hexagon

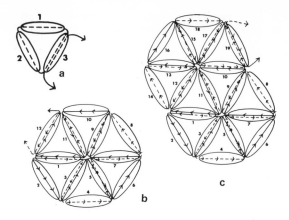

Illus. 8. Diagram for beaded mats. In a: the first three beads. In b: one completed hexagon. In c: two adjacent hexagons.

Illus. 9. These two beaded mats are made with the same technique, but the oval beads used in the mat on the right produce a much lighter appearance.

12

(Illus. 8b), the threads cross in beads 3, 5, 7, 9, 11, and 1. Beads 12, 11, and 10 of the first hexagon form spokes of the second hexagon as well. Beads 19, 10, 9 and 8 become spokes for the third hexagon.

The table mat in Illus. 9 uses beads of different colors: the middle hexagon, made with dark beads, is the first one which you make. The hexagons which surround this first one, the light group in the picture, are made in a circle around this first one. You can make the mat as large as

Illus. 10. In this necklace of hexagonal rosettes, hexagons are made together in groups of three— except for the three on the bottom, made separately from each other to give the proper curve to the necklace.

you want simply by adding another round of beads.

The other table mat shown in Illus. 9 uses exactly the same threading procedures as the first one does. It looks a bit fancier because of a simple extra step: before you place an oval bead on the thread, slip a round one on. The result is a mat much lighter in appearance and more loosely formed. While it covers the same area as the other mat, fewer hexagons are needed because the round beads expand each small triangle.

Necklace of Hexagonal Rosettes

The necklace in Illus. 10 uses the same threading techniques as the mats on page 12. The oval beads here are slightly smaller than the ones in the mats, and the round ones slightly larger, but as you can see by studying the picture, the design of the two pieces is similar.

Begin the threading by making half of a hexagon, and then, using the same cord, thread another hexagon to this half. Now you are ready to make the first group of three rosettes. Begin a new thread (the first one will not be in the proper position) by inserting it in the bottom bead of the hexagon you just completed. Make three hexagons together: the bottom two triangles of the first should be the top two triangles of the second (just like the threading technique for the mats, page 12), and the bottom two triangles of the second become the top two triangles of the third. After you make the third hexagon, end the thread by gluing it back into a nearby bead. Begin a new series of three rosettes by inserting a new thread through the bottom oval bead. By

13

making the hexagons in groups of three, you form the circular shape necessary for the necklace to go around your neck.

At the end of the necklace, make two hanging dangles with small beads and oval ones. To fasten the necklace, insert one of these long parts through a triangle of the half hexagon at the other end of the necklace, and twist the dangle around a few beads. Do the same with the other dangle and triangle, and the necklace will stay securely around your neck.

Beaded Headband
Using Macramé Technique

You can easily buy an attractive headband, but why not make your own instead? You can choose your own colors, save some money, and have the satisfaction of wearing your own creation. The headband on the right, while it does not use any macramé knots, is similar to macramé because of the cords which show. The waxed cord with beads strung on it goes around an inexpensive plastic headband that was first covered with ribbon. Large beads and thick cord make this headband a sporty accessory; artificial pearls or crystal beads strung on metallic thread would make a more formal hair ornament.

Buy a clear plastic headband and a piece of grosgrain ribbon (or satin ribbon, if you want a shiny finish) about half a yard long and twice as wide as the headband, plus $\frac{1}{2}''$. Before you begin your beadwork, cover the headband with the ribbon: place the ribbon lengthwise on top of the headband and turn the two side edges of the

Illus. 11. When you make your beaded headband, be sure to pull the cords tightly. Then the beads cannot roll or move from their proper position.

ribbon to the back of the headband. Slip-stitch the sides together firmly by hand. On each end of the band, cut off the extra length of ribbon, leaving about $\frac{1}{2}''$ on each end. Turn this $\frac{1}{2}''$ toward the inside of the ribbon and slip-stitch the ends in place.

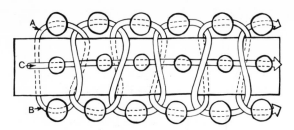

Illus. 12. Diagram for the beaded headband. The dotted lines are those parts of the cord which will not show.

Now you are ready to weave the beads and cord on the band. Follow the diagram here to understand the pattern. Attach the cord which winds over and under the band (A and B) first. When you attach cord C, it holds A and B in place more securely up the middle. Measure and cut a length of cord 10 times the length of the headband, for cords A and B. (This may seem very long, but remember that you first double the thread and then wind it over and under the band many times. Besides, it is better to have the cord too long than too short.) Fold the cord so you have two equal lengths, and place the fold under the band at one end. Bring both ends of the cord to the top of the band. With a needle and any kind of thread, make a small stitch to attach the cord to the ribbon on the underside of the band. Make sure the cord is attached securely; this stitch must bear the tension of the entire threading process.

Slide a bead on each cord and push them to the beginning. Take cord A (see Illus. 12) and place it loosely under the band. Bring cord B underneath A, and then over the top of the

band, and finally underneath A on the other side. Slide two more beads on the cords. Now bring B across the top of the band. Slip B under A, then cross A under the band and bring it through the space between the band and B. Continue beading and weaving in this way until you reach the end of the band. Notice that B is always the cord that lies on top of the band, while A is always on the underside.

When you reach the end of the band, fasten cords A and B to the ribbon. Tie A and B together on the underside of the band with a loose knot. With a needle and thread, take a small stitch to fasten the cords to the ribbon, as you did at the start of the band.

Now you are ready to weave the cord which runs up the middle of the band, C. Measure a piece of cord about 5″ longer than the band itself. If the cord is thin enough, thread a needle, tie a knot in one end of the cord, and insert the needle into the small margin of ribbon at the very end of the band. If the cord is too thick to be threaded, secure one end to the ribbon with small stitches made with another thread.

Place a bead on C and slide it to the end attached to the ribbon. Slip the cord under the one which crosses the top of the band (B). Continue placing beads on C and threading C under B until you reach the other end of the band. Fasten cord C the same way you began it. The diagram showing all these cords may look complicated to you, but remember that the dotted lines represent cords which do not show on the headband itself. The finished piece has just enough beadwork and cord showing to make a simple yet elegant accessory.

Beads plus Embroidery

Both macramé and embroidery with beads incorporate the thread or cord holding the beads together as part of the design. Embroidery requires a needle to fasten the beads to an already prepared backing, while macramé uses heavy string to make objects from scratch. Because embroidery decorates while macramé constructs, embroidery is the easier technique to learn. By making embroidered and beaded motifs, you become familiar with the tricky process of threading the beads on a cord or string. The background you embroider on makes it easy to see what you are doing. Once you can successfully work with the beads plus embroidery technique, you can progress to beads plus macramé with confidence.

Study the illustrations and try to reproduce them. Embroidering on a fabric which is loosely woven or has a regular pattern in it is easier than working on a closely woven material; the threads or lines in the loose fabric act as guides to keep your stitches straight and even. On plain material with no such guides, add light lines with tailor's chalk to help you.

Be sure to use beads which have sufficiently large holes, as sometimes in an intricate pattern the thread passes through the hole several times. The type of bead you use matters also: on tablecloths and other things to be laundered, use only glass, ceramic or plastic beads, never wood ones. The finish on the wood will flake from the heat of the water and detergent. You can use wood beads on other articles, but use thick wool yarn instead of fine silk or cotton thread.

Some Embroidery Stitches

Running Stitch

The running stitch is the most basic stitch, not only in embroidery but in any needlecraft. Bring the needle from the wrong side to the right side of your fabric. Now, take a stitch by inserting the needle in the fabric through to the wrong side and bringing it through to the right side again. Pull the thread through the fabric until it lies flat, and you have made one running stitch. The stitches should be neat and evenly spaced. The space between two stitches can be either longer or shorter than the stitch itself, for interesting effects.

You can vary the running stitch in a number of ways, and add beads to the stitching as you do. The beads will sparkle against the solid background and show off your stitching. The easiest variation is the *threaded running stitch*, diagrammed in Illus. 13a. Using a contrasting color

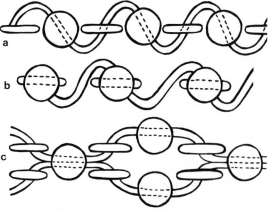

Illus. 13. Threaded running stitch and variations.

for the winding thread, slip the needle—with beads strung on it if you want—under the running stitches. To prevent the beads from sliding around on the thread after you complete the stitching, make the running stitches close together and use beads which are large enough to fill in the spaces between the running stitches. Or, thread the beads on the running stitch itself (Illus. 13b). The best way to determine which style is best for your threads, beads and fabric is, of course, to make small samples with the materials you plan to use.

Another variation, seen in Illus. 13c, uses two parallel rows of running stitches that are connected by two threads which wind between the rows. Place a bead on the winding thread before you put the needle under each running stitch. Do not make stitches in the fabric with the winding thread; the running stitches hold the thread and beads securely enough, and even small stitches would attach the beads too tightly.

Chevron Stitch

The chevron stitch looks like two parallel rows of running stitches with a third thread winding between the rows. Actually, however, you make this stitch with just one thread. Follow Illus. 14 closely, beginning at A and ending at H. First practice making a few chevron stitches using only embroidery floss or fine crewel wool; then string some beads on the thread and experiment to see which placement you prefer. See the illustration for the possibilities and combinations.

Y Stitch

The Y stitch, so called because it looks like the letter Y, is a stitch you will frequently use. It is very easy to make, and the variations, which depend upon the length of the stem of the Y, are no more complicated than the basic stitch itself.

Follow the diagram in Illus. 15a: starting at A, insert the needle through to the wrong side of

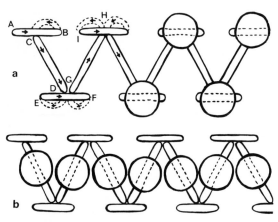

Illus. 14. Chevron stitch and variations.

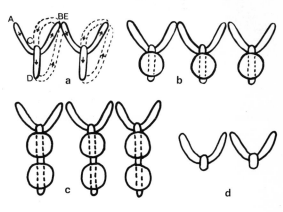

Illus. 15. The Y stitch and variations. The stitch diagrammed in d is called the "fly stitch."

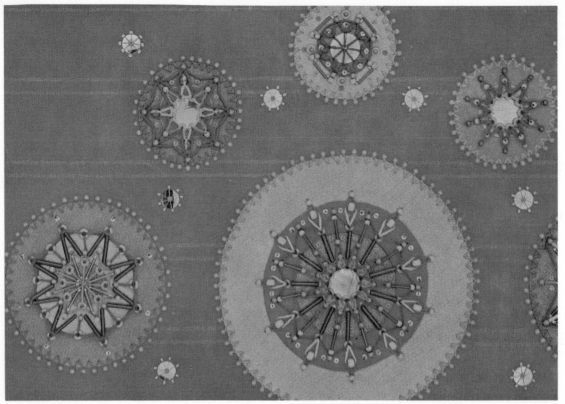

Illus. 16. A colorful assortment of geometric motifs embroidered randomly on a piece of fabric. Sequins and beads between the circles add sparkle to this wall hanging.

the fabric at B, and back to the right side at C. Do not pull stitch A-B tightly; leave it loose enough to form the curved part of the Y. Insert the needle to the wrong side at D, and as you tighten the stitch C-D, pull the loop which extends from A to B so it lies flat on the fabric. Bring the needle up near B at E, and you are ready to make another stitch.

For variety, place a bead on the thread before you make the stem (C-D) of the Y. You can make the stem very long and use two or even three beads, perhaps of different sizes. Or, make the stem very short—just big enough to catch the loop A-B—to make the *fly stitch*.

The Y stitch when used alone makes an attractive border, but you might want to combine it with other stitches to make a more solid and elaborate area.

Illus. 17. A plain leather handbag or change purse can benefit from a unique embroidered and beaded design. See page 27 for instructions for sewing on leather.

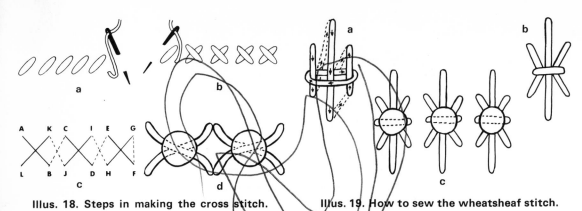

Illus. 18. Steps in making the cross stitch.

Illus. 19. How to sew the wheatsheaf stitch.

Cross Stitch

The cross stitch is one of the most commonly used stitches, because the regularity of the stitches makes it easy to achieve precise, geometric embroidery. To make the basic cross stitch, first work all diagonals in one direction down the row. (See Illus. 18.) Then finish the crosses by turning the work and crossing each diagonal. By stitching all the diagonals in a row at one time, rather than each stitch individually, you are sure to make them evenly. The same half-stitch will be the top stitch on every cross.

To make the cross stitch with beads attached, place a bead on the thread each time you are about to insert the needle through to the wrong side of the fabric while you make the first diagonal stitches. When you return across the row to finish the crosses, insert the needle through the bead again before you put the needle in the fabric.

Wheatsheaf Stitch

For all its spectacular effects, the basic wheatsheaf stitch is not hard to do: make three parallel stitches, the middle one longer than the others. Bring the needle up in the center of the longest stitch, but do not split the thread. Then take the needle behind one of the shorter stitches, around and over all three, behind the other short stitch and back into the fabric. Pull the thread tightly so that the stitches on the side are pulled toward the middle. The finished stitch looks like a bundle of wheat tied at the middle. (See Illus. 19.)

A sparkling bead on the horizontal thread changes the whole appearance of this stitch. The pulled side stitches now look like beams radiating from the bead. For extra sheen, use a crystal or glass bead and metallic thread. This stitch makes an elegant edging along a collar or neck, or even along the hem of a garment.

20

Miscellaneous Stitches

Some stitches are common and have been given names throughout the years. New ones are constantly being invented, however; embroidery, while an ancient craft, changes with the times just as any form of art does. If you happen upon a new stitch as you sew, you might want to look it up in a complete embroidery handbook to find out if it has been done before, and if it has a name. Rather than being disappointed if you don't find it, you should be delighted: you have invented a new stitch! Use it often and let it become your own signature on your embroidery.

Some of the stitches which appear here were discovered this way, and although they might have names in one handbook or another, the embroidress preferred to think of them as her own and so left them unnamed. Study the illustrations to see how the stitches were made, and then use your own needle, thread and imagination to design original stitches.

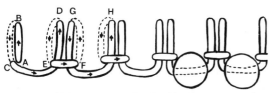

Illus. 20. When you made the Y stitch, you left a loop of thread on the surface of the fabric. Do the same thing here: make a small stitch from A to B, and bring the needle up at C. Then curve the thread so that it forms the loop CD, and hold the curve flat with the horizontal stitch EF. Bring the needle up at G, pass it under EF, and curve the thread around to H. To hold the curve securely so it does not pull up, place a bead on the lower part of the curve.

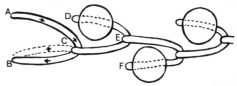

Illus. 21. In this stitch you again make loops with the thread rather than pull it straight. Starting at A, make a loose loop and insert the needle to the wrong side at B. Then bring the needle up inside the loop at C. Make the second stitch curve to the other side. (In other words, D should be along the same line as A, while E and C should be points in the middle of the line of stitches.)

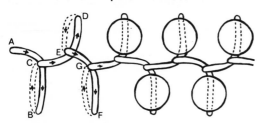

Illus. 22. A variation of Illus. 21 has slightly curved threads instead of sharp loops. This stitch covers a wider surface than that in Illus. 21.

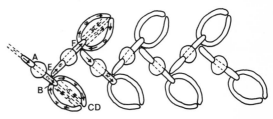

Illus. 23. Take a stitch from A to B and bring the needle up at C. Curve the thread by passing the needle under the stitch AB, insert the needle in the fabric right next to C at D, and bring it up again at E, behind the curve CD.

21

Embroidery on Cloth

Border on a Bathrobe

Now that you have experimented and made a few embroidered and beaded samples, use your knowledge to add an elegant decoration to a piece of clothing. The little girl on page 23 is wearing a bright red flannel bathrobe, which was first made by hand and then decorated with embroidery and beads along the border of the closing and the top of the pocket. You too can make and decorate a bathrobe like this, or apply the same technique to decorate any piece of clothing or home furnishing, such as a tablecloth or bureau scarf.

The close-up view of the pocket border in Illus. 24 shows more clearly what stitches to use. Embroider the border on the pocket before you attach the pocket to the bathrobe, as it is easier to handle a small piece than a large one. First attach a border of felt or woven binding to the edge of the pocket. If you use felt, cut a piece twice as wide as you want the border to be, and fold it over the edge of the pocket. Woven binding usually comes already folded in half. Stitch the border to the pocket either by hand or by machine.

Use fine wool yarn rather than embroidery floss for the embroidery in this project, so that the thread shows up on the nappy flannel. Save your embroidery floss for linen tablecloths or cotton fabrics. Embroider a few rows of overcast stitches with the wool along the edge of the binding, and then arrange your beads in front of you according to color and size.

You should plan your design and mark off the proper spacing on the pocket before you start to embroider. The pocket here, diagrammed in Illus. 26, is symmetrical. There are 13 beads on 13 running stitches in the first row of stitching. Mark off 13 equally spaced points on the pocket, so that you will know where to stitch. Once you have marked and attached these 13 beads, you can stitch around them and not have to measure or mark the pocket again.

The light stitches in the diagram are Y stitches with two beads on each stem. Make the Y stitches so the top of the Y is in-between two of the 13 beads which you just attached with the running stitch. Make seven Y stitches, one for every other one of the original 13 beads. Set off the other six beads by six stitches in a darker color, made

Illus. 24. This close-up of the pocket border in Illus. 25 shows the left side of the pocket.

Illus. 25. Warm and cozy in her hand-decorated flannel bathrobe, this little girl plays on without worrying about catching a chill.

23

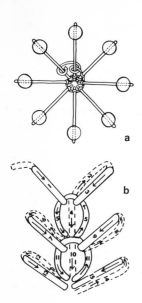

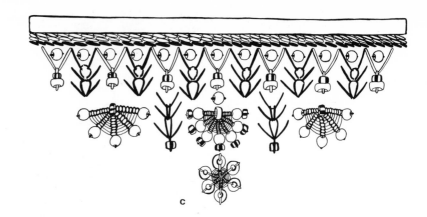

Illus. 26. In a: forming a "cobweb." This cobweb has eight spokes, as the one below the front closing of the robe does. The principle is the same no matter how many spokes there are. In b: the "ear of corn" stitch. In c: diagram of the pocket border, based on 13 beads.

similarly to the Y stitches, but with more branches and loops. See Illus. 26b for the diagram of this stitch.

Under the third stitch from each end of the border, make the looped arrangement called a "cobweb." Make five straight stitches radiating from one point to form a semi-circle, and fasten a bead in the middle of the circle and at the end of each stitch. Loop yarn around each stitch (see Illus. 26a) until the entire area, from the middle bead to the ones at the tips of the stitches, is "webbed" with wool. Make the cobweb in the middle exactly the same way, only make seven straight stitches instead of five, and attach two beads to the end of each stitch. Make the small circular cobweb under the seven-spoked one by attaching round beads flat to the fabric so the holes point up.

Try your hand designing your own borders, using the stitches you have learned here or inventing your own. As long as your design is symmetrical in both stitching and color, it will probably be attractive. Decorate collars, the yoke of a dress, the edge of a tablecloth or even the hem of your curtains. Remember to match your thread or yarn to the cloth on which you are stitching for the best results.

Embroidered and Beaded Wall Hanging

Wall hangings lend themselves to a great deal of personal expression. They can be either simple or complex, depending upon both your skill as an embroidress and your desire for a rich motif. If you can make the basic running stitch, you can make a beautiful wall hanging.

Illus. 27. While each of these embroidered motifs is similar due to the geometric arrangement, there is actually an infinite variety of possible designs. A mural such as this, composed of different designs, still has an underlying harmony.

The embroidered mural in Illus. 27 is the work of a group of students, each of whom was given beads, thread, three pieces of felt, and a piece of cotton cloth for the background. They worked independently, but the geometric theme of each of their designs gives unity to the finished hanging. A design with a definite mid-point on which the eye can focus, with lines radiating from this point, is almost always pleasing to look at because of the rhythmic and balanced composition. A

geometric pattern is a good design for a beginner to work with, for you can practice your stitches while the design almost forms itself. Try your hand at creating a wall hanging similar to this, composed either of several small squares stitched together to form a patchwork design, or make one large but elaborate motif.

Choose your thread, beads and background colors before you decide on a pattern. The types of materials you buy will help you plan your design: if you buy wood beads and wool thread, for example, arrange the beads and thread with more open spaces than if you choose fine silk thread and tiny crystal beads. Remember also that the color of the background makes a big difference in the effect of the finished project. Yellows, oranges and reds are warm colors and greatly enhance a room which receives little sunlight. Blues, greens and purples, on the other hand, are cooler. Place them in a room which is already bright enough but which needs a relaxing element such as a soothing wall hanging. You can of course effectively mix the two families of color; see page 18 for a wall hanging which basically uses warm colors but has spots of green and blue for contrast.

After you have decided on a color for the background, choose felt which harmonizes with that color. Cut three circles, each one smaller than the last, and glue them on top of each other. Now you are ready to plan the design on paper.

Use a compass or trace a round object on plain paper to form a circle about the same size as the largest piece of felt. Draw the two smaller circles inside this large one, and then mark off the proper number of areas in the circle, depending on the number of times you want to repeat your design. It is easy to divide the circle in half, then in quarters, and then in eighths, but if you want to make a design based on sixths, tenths or some other number, use a protractor.

Divide 360° (the number of degrees in a circle) by the number of areas you want, to find the number of degrees that each area should be. For example, if you want a pattern based on sixths, divide 360 by 6 to get 60, the number of degrees in one-sixth of a circle. Draw a line from the middle of the circle to the edge to represent 0° and 360°, and use the protractor to measure from this line. At the proper degree mark, draw a line to the middle of the circle. Measure again from this second line, and continue in this manner around the circle until you reach the first line.

Decide on the arrangement of beads and thread now, so that when you begin stitching you do not have to stop to decide what color to use next. Of course the design you plan now is not binding; if as you stitch you find a more attractive arrangement, by all means use it rather than the pattern you sketched. Planning the colors and types of beads on paper will, however, remind you what color to use, which bead belongs where, and what type of stitch should attach the bead. The pattern guarantees symmetry, since you can follow it for each section to avoid using the wrong thread on one part.

While you do not have to draw the entire design on the felt circles before you stitch, use tailor's chalk at least to mark off the right number of areas. Then begin your embroidery with beads, fastening the beads securely and taking care to make the stitches neat and attractive. Complete all the stitching you can before you attach the felt to the cotton. If you plan to use a lot of stitching around the large felt circle, this is usually sufficient to hold the felt securely to the cotton. If, however, the stitching is simple and there are not many points where the felt is attached to the cotton, it is best to attach the felt with an invisible hem stitch before you add the decorative top stitching.

Embroidery on Leather

Leather Handbag (see page 19)

Now that you are experienced with creating and executing embroidered designs on cloth and have practiced by making a wall hanging, why not try to decorate something more useful? A drab leather handbag may need only your creative talents to turn it into a fancy accessory. The handbag and coin purse on page 19 were decorated just as the wall hanging was. Sewing on leather does require a bit more care and a few more special materials than ordinary cloth, but it is certainly no more difficult nor expensive than what you have already done.

Use an old leather handbag that needs rejuvenating, or buy a new one that has no decoration. Choose smooth leather rather than suede, as suede soils easily. Leather and hobby shops sell leather remnants by the pound so you should have little difficulty in finding the right materials to work with. Choose your colors as carefully for this leather ornament as you did for

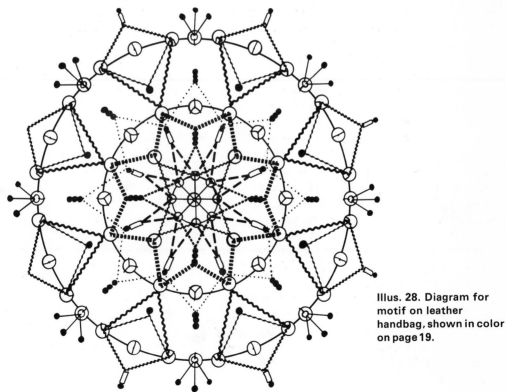

Illus. 28. Diagram for motif on leather handbag, shown in color on page 19.

the wall hanging, keeping in mind the occasions you plan to use the bag and the colors of your wardrobe.

Sewing on leather requires a strong needle with a thick eye. When you push the needle into the leather, the eye will make a hole larger than the thread, and enable you to pull the thread through after the needle without any trouble. Use buttonhole silk when you sew on leather. It is strong, has an attractive sheen, and comes in all colors.

To make the leather ornament, follow the same steps as the decoration for the wall hanging. Using a sharp pocketknife or a single-edged razor blade in a holder, carefully cut out the leather circles to the size you want. Glue the circles together with rubber cement or special leather glue, and then stitch the pattern you have planned. The diagram of the pattern for the leather handbag on page 19 is in Illus 28. Follow it if you want to copy that pattern, or design your own on paper.

Use a variety of beads of different shapes. Glass bars and sequins on the pictured handbag add interest, as well as more sparkle than just round beads can give. Choose the beads themselves as carefully as you choose the colors, for they can greatly add to or detract from the finished pattern.

Leather-Covered Box (see page 11)

The leather pieces which decorate the box on page 11 are ornately embroidered with stitching and beads. Cover a box with decorated leather pieces to sit on a bureau or coffee table as an attractive jewelry box or cigarette case. If you prefer not to work with leather, or if the style of your room is more suited to another material,

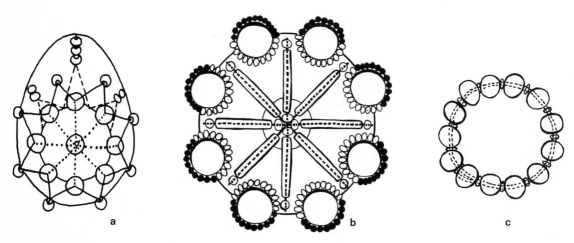

a   b   c

Illus. 29. Diagrams for motif on leather-covered box, shown in color on page 11. In a: the maroon ovals. In b: the center dark green circle. In c: the small blue rings which surround the large orange beads.

you can also decorate pieces of fabric and attach them to the box just as you would attach leather.

Use a small metal box, the kind which holds candy or loose tea. The metal guarantees a long-lasting piece, so your decorative efforts will last and make it worth both the money and energy you invest. Covering a box with leather—or felt, vinyl or velvet, if you use one of these materials—requires careful measuring and placement of both material and beads.

Just as you did in the other projects, plan your design on paper before you begin stitching. The design on the box in Illus. 7 is diagrammed here; follow it or plan a new one. This project is made of many small pieces of leather glued on top of each other, with a large spangle in the middle. The pieces must be the exact size. Draw the pattern on paper in the size that the finished box will be, and place the pattern over the leather. Then cut out the leather pieces with your knife or razor blade by cutting around the paper. Make continuous, even cuts with one stroke of the blade to avoid a ragged edge.

Because leather is a thick material, and because there is not much sewing involved here, buy a good non-staining glue made for leather. Begin by glueing the smallest piece—the light blue-green spangle—to the dark green leather circle, and mark off the circle into eighths. Then sew the light blue beads and brown glass bars to this piece along those markings. Glue the dark green circle to the larger moss green piece, pressing and smoothing it from the middle to the edges so that it lies flat. Glue the large orange beads to the leather between the glass bars, and prepare the rings surrounding the orange beads.

The only way to determine how many beads are needed for the ring is to string several and wrap them around the large bead to see if they are enough. When you have established the number, make eight rings with half light blue beads and half dark blue. Slip a ring around an orange bead and take small stitches between each bead on the ring to hold it in place on the leather (see Illus. 29c). The stitches are invisible and also hold the two leather circles together more securely.

Now you are ready to glue the moss green circle to the orange leather which will cover the top of the box. Make the orange piece larger than the top so that it overlaps the edge by $\frac{1}{2}''$ (that is, the diameter of the orange circle should be $1''$ larger than that of the top itself), and glue the green leather to the middle of the orange. Cut eight red egg-shaped pieces and sew the large light blue spangles and the smaller sequins which surround them to the red pieces. Glue these leather shapes on top of the orange and green circles in line with the glass bars. Attach the rest of the beads—the dark blue ones between the red pieces, and those beads surrounding the red shapes—by sewing, not glueing. Make sure they are securely fastened, but avoid any extra threads on the underside of the orange leather. Dangling threads make it difficult to glue the orange leather smoothly to the metal.

Make sure that the metal is clean of any grease or dirt before you attach the leather. Center the orange leather on the lid, with all the beading and embroidery completed, and firmly smooth and stretch it from the middle to the edge. Brush glue on the sides of the lid also, and press the $\frac{1}{2}''$-

hem of leather down firmly on this area. Cut another piece of orange leather to go around the side of the lid, to cover the edge of the ornament and give a more finished and professional appearance to your work. Make the piece as long as the circumference of the lid, and as wide as the side of the lid plus $\frac{1}{2}''$. Before you attach this strip, turn in and glue $\frac{1}{4}''$ on each edge. Then brush glue on both the edge of the box and the strip, and place the two pieces together. Smooth and press the leather strip with your fingers as you did the top piece, and the lid of your box is completed.

Cover the bottom portion, if the lid does not reach completely down the sides. Place the lid on the bottom of the box and measure the height of the area that is not covered by the lid. Cut a strip as wide as this measurement plus $\frac{1}{2}''$, and as long as the circumference of the box. Glue the strip to the bottom just as you glued the strip around the edge of the top, and turn the extra $\frac{1}{2}''$ width to the underside of the bottom of the box. You should not cover the container bottom with leather all the way to the top edge, because the extra thickness does not permit the top to fit on the bottom. When the box is closed, all the parts that show are covered with leather—attached and decorated by you.

Basic Macramé Techniques

Macramé is a technique of knotting, using thick thread, cord, yarn or string. It was originally practiced in southern Europe during the late Middle Ages, and has been enthusiastically revived during the past few years. Besides being a simple and therefore popular craft, macramé is quite fashionable to wear. The objects made with macramé knots—either with beads or without—are attractive and stylish, but they are not at all difficult to do. Macramé knots are simply the ordinary knots which you tie every day arranged in a decorative order.

You need a working base on which to anchor your knotting as you proceed. A firm pillow or the upholstered arm of a chair is suitable. Secure your knotting to this base with pins or thumbtacks, so that as you knot you can pull tightly without dislodging the entire article you are making. Have on hand a pair of scissors, a variety of cord and twine, a tape measure and a crochet hook, to pull loose ends through to the wrong side of your work. After learning the basic knots, gather an assortment of beads together—large ones with wide holes are best—to embellish and add sparkle to your work.

HINT FOR MACRAMÉ:

To determine how long to cut the cords, work a sample about 3 inches square, using the same pattern stitch and cord which you are going to use in your project. Divide the length of cord you used in the sample by 3, to determine how much cord is used in 1 square inch, and multiply that number by the number of square inches there will be in your finished project. If the design is a loose one with few knots, it might use strands only 3 times the length of the completed article (so you would cut cords 6 times the project's length, and fold them in half), while if your design is very dense it might require 5 or 6 times (doubled) the length of the project.

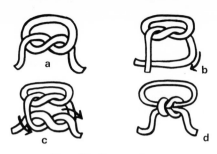

Illus. 35. Square knot.

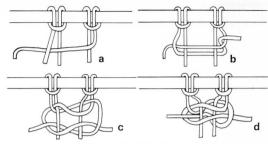

Illus. 36. Flat knot.

Square and Flat Knots

The square knot (SK) is made by interlacing two cords. Follow Illus. 35 as you read these instructions: Place the left cord under the right. Bring the right cord up through the loop just made, and pull the end of the right cord through (a). Now, reverse direction: place the right cord (that is, what is *now* the right cord) under the left, and pull the left cord through the loop (b–c). Pull both ends evenly (d).

The square knot has several variations, the most common of which is the *flat knot* (FK). Make the flat knot in exactly the same way as the square knot, only tie each half knot around two cords. (See Illus. 36.) These cords do not form any part of the knot itself; they just hang and make the knot more prominent.

Many square or flat knots made one right after the other with the same two or four cords form a "sennit." Sennits are frequently used as transitional patterns between groups of diagonal and horizontal bars (see page 47), while individual square and flat knots loosely connect strands for a lacy effect. Turn to the covered bottle on page 36 for an example of this type of knotting.

Simple Beaded Belt

Combining beads with the macramé knots you have learned should come quite naturally to you, now that you have both embroidered with beads and practiced macramé. The belt in Illus. 37 is a good project for you to start with: it uses both DK's and FK's, and looks much more intricate than it really is. The pleasing result will spur you on to make the more complex articles pictured in this book.

The main portion of the belt is Diag. DK bars, while the thin portion is a sennit of FK's. Start the knotting by mounting cords on a foundation knot bearer (Fnd. KB) of a cord 6 inches long:

a. Mount a cord about one-third from the end of the 6-inch Fnd. KB.

b. Slide a bead on the Fnd. KB from the longer side.

c. Mount another cord next to this bead.

d. Place another bead on the Fnd. KB.

e. Take the inside strand of the cord you just mounted in *c* and loop it above and back to the Fnd. KB. Make a double knot with this cord on the Fnd. KB, so that the end of the cord hangs down as the fourth strand.

Illus. 37. A belt made of beads plus macramé. The construction is simple but the results are unusual.

f. Place another bead on the Fnd. KB.

g. Mount another double cord next to this bead.

(When you have completed the belt, you will curl the ends of the Fnd. KB through the loop you made in *e*, and attach them with stitching to the wrong side. Do not do this until the knotting is

completed, or you will not have a Fnd. KB to pin to your working base.)

Using the two outside strands as KB's, make Diag. DK bars toward the middle. You make two knots over each KB, as there are four strands besides the KB's. When the KB's meet in the center, do not knot them as you did on page 32.

Instead, insert each through a bead, and then complete the cross by making two more knots on each KB. Before you make the last knot on each side, slide two beads on each strand. At this point in your work, there is one set of diagonal double knot bars with a bead in the center of the cross and two beads on each side. Make 13 crosses of the Diag. DK bars.

Place one bead on each of the KB's, and then make a DK on each KB with the two inside strands. Let the other two strands hang loose for the time being. The KB's are now the two strands in the middle of the belt. Using those strands which you just used to make the DK's, make successive FK's around the KB's. Make the sennit long enough so the belt is your waist measurement plus at least 4 or 5 inches.

When you have made the sennit long enough, place three beads on each of the inside cords (that is, the former KB's). Turn these ends away from the center, and stitch them to the underside of the sennit. Fasten the other two ends also with stitches, or pull them through nearby knots with a crochet hook.

The two strands still hang loose where the sennit begins. Pull these through one of the first FK's to the wrong side, and fasten with stitches. Do not forget to do the same to the ends of the Fnd. KB at the mounting.

To wear the belt, slip the sennit through the loop at the other end. Pull until it is as tight as you want, and then loop the sennit in and out of the first set of Diag. DK bars. The beads at the end of the sennit form a large knob which keeps the belt from unfastening.

Covered Bottle

Macramé is made of flexible cords, so you can knot around three-dimensional objects. A covered bottle is a simple project, besides being attractive and practical. You knot the cords right on the bottle itself, so the cover closely surrounds the glass shape. Rescue an ordinary wine bottle or a jar of an unusual shape from the garbage and decorate it for a sparkling and original ornament. The front cover shows several possible designs for covered bottles and jars, which you can easily copy. The cover on the bottle in Illus. 38 is an easy design to make, and after practicing with its simple pattern, you should be inspired to try more intricate knots.

The Fnd. KB for a covered bottle is a cord. Thread a number of beads divisible by four on the cord (12 or 16 beads is customary, depending on the circumference of the bottle and the size of the beads) and tie the cord around the neck of the bottle or jar. Do not place too many beads on the Fnd. KB or there will not be enough space to mount the knotting cords. Mount one (double) cord between every two beads, as diagrammed in Illus. 39a. Now you are ready to begin the macramé knotting.

Every bead has two strands on each side of it. You are about to make FK sennits, which use *four* strands. Following Illus. 39b, pick up one strand (a) and bring it under the bead it is next to; then pick up the strand on the other side of the adjacent bead (d) and bring it to the first strand. These two strands, a and d, are those with which you tie the FK's, while the two middle strands, b and c, are those which hang through the

Illus. 38. Bottles covered with beads plus macramé are among the most unique gift items you can give. See the front cover for some other elegant examples.

of four. Now regroup the sets of four in the following way: take strands d and a from adjacent groups of four and insert the ends into a dark bead, from opposite ends of the bead. These two strands are the center strands in the new group of four, while strand c, next to that d, and strand b, next to that a, are the outside strands which form knots. Tie FK sennits with the new groups of strands—lettered c–d–a–b—as long as you want.

After you have made these FK sennits, thread more beads on the strands as you just did, crossing the strands so that the original groups of four are back together. Tie FK's with a and d, and allow b and c to hang down the center of the sennit.

To form the criss-cross pattern on the bottle in Illus. 38, alternate your knotting threads, first making FK knots all around the bottle with a and d, and then switching to c and b. Add beads wherever it pleases you and make sennits rather than one knot if it looks attractive on your bottle.

Securing the strands on the bottom of the bottle is an important step in making this cover, for it holds them correctly in place on the entire bottle. Turn the bottle upside down and hold it between your knees as you work. Tie strands from opposite sides of the bottle with square knots, but do not cut the ends off. Next, tie adjacent strands together, also with square knots. Continue tying square knots until every strand is connected to at least one other, and cut the ends off. When you make the knots, avoid large lumps, so the bottle can stand flat on a table. Glue the knots to the bottom of the bottle with a clear-drying glue if they do not lie flat against the glass.

middle of the sennit. Knot FK sennits as long as you want with each group of four cords.

Slip a clear bead on strands a and d of each set

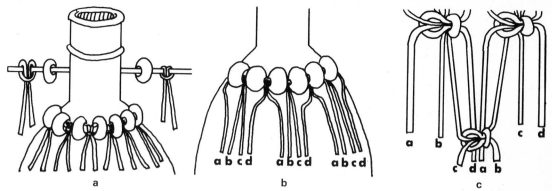

Illus. 39. In a: mounting cords on the Fnd. KB. In b: the four cords which make the first flat knot. In c: the four cords rearranged to make the next flat knot.

Jewelry with Beads

Primitive man wore necklaces and bracelets made out of cord and bits of shell or bone, knotted together in the ways you are learning here. The cords that you use for jewelry can be thinner than those you use for objects subject to more stress, and the cords can then go through the small beads easily. Making jewelry with macramé demands agility and even knotting. To acquaint yourself with the technique of jewelry-making before adding macramé knots, try the pendant in Illus. 40 first.

Woven Necklace (see next page)

By sliding beads on one thread and then weaving them around other perpendicular threads, you can quickly and easily fill in the solid areas of this necklace. Design a pattern on graph paper with squares the same size as one bead. Fill in each square with colored pencil to show which color bead should lie over that square.

Paste this graph paper to a piece of cardboard slightly larger on all sides than the finished pendant is to be, and punch 14 holes across the top of the cardboard, separated by the distance of one bead. Cut seven cords twice the length of the pendant, plus 2". From the wrong side of the cardboard, insert each end of these lengthwise cords through the holes you just punched. Holding these cords taut, slide the little beads and long glass bars on them to their approximate positions. Punch holes in the bottom of the cardboard as you did at the top, insert the ends of the cords through these holes, and tie every pair together on the wrong side of the cardboard.

Now you are ready to weave the solid area of beads. Thread a darning needle with sturdy thread—heavy-duty or nylon thread is a good choice—and secure it to the top right corner of the pendant with several small stitches or knots. Slide 13 beads on the thread according to the

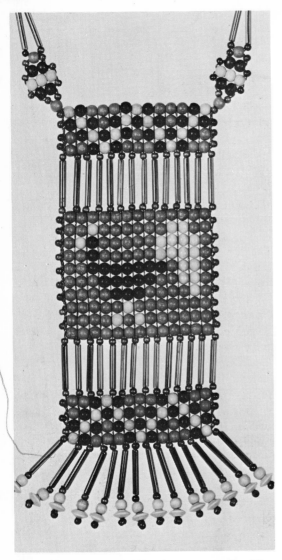

colors you marked on the graph paper. Draw the entire row of beads *under* the lengthwise threads at the top of the pendant. Place a small bead on the needle and bring the needle around the long thread on the side, through the end bead again and into the row of beads, on *top* of the 14 threads, back to the starting point. Place another small bead on the needle. Thread 13 more beads on the string for the next row, and weave it as you did the first row.

When you have woven all the rows, carefully tear the cardboard away from the beads. Remove it gently, as you don't want to break any threads. Untie the knots you made with the pairs of lengthwise cords and place a few beads on the end of each string. Instead of tying bulky knots on each end, turn the threads back into the beads and secure with a few drops of clear glue.

To hang the pendant around your neck, you must attach it to long pieces which will tie in the back. Use any attractive arrangement of beads, and make two identical pieces. Fasten them securely to each top corner of the beaded rectangle, and your pendant is complete.

Illus. 40. A woven necklace is easy to make. Plan your colors on graph paper before you begin.

Necklace of
Beads plus Macramé

Jewelry which combines both sparkling bead-work and intricate knotting is the ultimate in ornate fashion accessories. The necklaces and pendants on pages 1 and 40 are examples of the fancy designs you should now be able to imitate. To get you started on this type of work, follow the instructions here to make the necklace on the left in Illus. 42. Examine the other designs closely

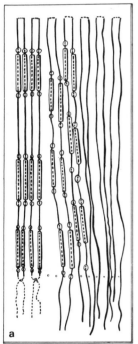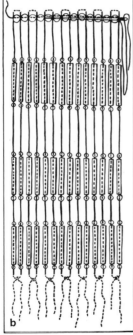

Illus. 41. Diagram of woven necklace. In a: stringing glass bars on the lengthwise threads. In b: weaving the first row behind the threads.

if you want to copy the pieces here, or mount several cords and begin knotting an original pattern. If you do choose to make your own design, remember that symmetrical designs are usually most pleasing.

Instructions for necklace on left in Illus. 42: First make the long pieces for tying. Slip 13 beads on two long cords and slide the beads to the middle. Use four different shapes and/or colors of beads. Assign each type of bead a letter, and arrange them on the cords in the order of

A–B–C–D–C–D–B–D–C–D–C–B–A.

Actually, any order is satisfactory, but when you use certain beads in specific places on the rest of the necklace, they will harmonize best if you begin with this order of beads. Alternate SK sennits with glass bars on each side of the 13 beads for the design on the ties.

Mount eight cords between the middle nine beads (there are, then, 16 strands for knotting). Make four FK sennits, two FK knots in each, with four groups of four strands each.

Slide an A bead on every strand which was a knotting strand (as opposed to a hanging strand). Make a sennit of two SK's with the two end strands on each side, and make three FK sennits of two FK's each with the 12 strands in the middle.

Slide an A bead on every hanging strand and make four FK sennits, each two FK's long.

Slide an A bead on every knotting strand. Make one SK with the two strands on each end, and divide the middle 12 strands into three groups of four strands. With each group, make one FK.

Let the middle four strands hang loose as you work with the six strands on each side. The

Illus. 42. Two examples of necklaces made with beads plus macramé. Instructions for the necklace on the left begin on page 39.

directions here tell you how to work with one side, but naturally they apply to both sides. For the most symmetrical results, work both sides at the same time.

Slide a glass bar on the strand second from the end and one on the strand fifth from the end.

The glass bars then have a strand on each side, as well as a strand through the center. Make one FK at the bottom of each glass bar, using only *one* hanging strand (the one which goes through the bar) instead of the usual two. Slide an A bead on each of the first two strands from the end.

Using the outside strand as KB, make a Diag. DK bar by tying DK's with the next two strands. Then, using what is *now* the outside strand, make another Diag. DK bar, tying knots with the next two strands (the second knotting strand is the KB of the first Diag. DK bar).

Place a D bead on the first and third strands. Make two more Diag. DK bars as before.

Slide one C bead on all three strands. Make one FK, with the middle strand hanging and the two on each side of it (#1 and #3) as knotting strands.

Separate the three strands by sliding five A beads on each. Tie a knot; then slide a C bead on each strand, and tie enough knots so the beads cannot slip off the strand. Clip off any excess string.

Now you are ready to complete the middle portion of the necklace. Taking the center four strands, slide three A beads on each of the outer strands of this group of four. Slide a B bead on the center two strands. Make two FK's with these four strands.

Repeat the last paragraph once. The middle portion should now be as long as the glass bars on the sides.

Pick up the three strands from each side which you left hanging after attaching the glass bars. Slide an A bead on the first and third of these three strands (on both sides of the center portion, of course). Make two Diag. DK bars with these three strands as you did before.

Now group all ten center strands together. Use the middle two strands as KB's for the first set of Diag. DK bars. Then use what have become the center strands as KB's for the *next* set of bars, and use the previous KB's as knotting strands. Do the same at the end of the second bar.

Slide one C bead on the middle two strands, and a D bead on each of the outer strands.

Using these outer strands as KB's, make three sets of closed Diag. DK bars toward the middle. Drop the KB of the first set of bars and pick up the next outer strand as KB as you did above.

Slide one A bead on the first two strands and one A bead on the next two strands. Make three sets of Diag. DK bars toward the middle again. When a KB from the left side reaches the middle, insert it through a C bead. Do the same from the right.

Let the ten strands hang loose. Knot the two middle ones once under the C bead. Tie a knot in each of the ten strands, then place an A bead on each. Then tie another knot, slide another A bead, and finish the strands with a large enough group of knots to prevent the beads from sliding off. Clip the ends of the strings.

Other Macramé Projects

There are virtually hundreds of things you can make with macramé knots: wall hangings, handbags, belts, bracelets, fringes for rugs or upholstered furniture, place mats—even vests,

Illus. 43. If you want to practice on a small project, try one of the ideas shown here. On the left, an eyeglass chain; in the middle, an ornament for a watch; on the right, a chain to hold a pencil.

ties, skirts or free-standing sculptures. This section only briefly describes the projects pictured on the next few pages. You should not need detailed instructions, because by now you are experienced enough with macramé and familiar with the appearance of the knots to be able to copy macramé objects by closely studying the pictures.

If you want to make only a small project, try one of the trinkets seen in Illus. 43. The eyeglass chain and pencil string use the same knotting technique: attach four strands of cord to the plastic caps which fit the ends of the eyeglasses and pencil (you can buy these in craft and hobby shops). Then thread beads on the strands, sometimes sliding the beads on all four, sometimes only on the middle two, and sometimes on each of the outer strands. Flat knots between the beads keep them from moving around on the cord.

The fancy piece attached to the watch, also in Illus. 43, is quite simple to make. Begin by mounting one cord on the watch handle, and then add beads and knots. To join more cords, mount them through the knots with the help of a crochet hook. Finish by making a small loop of beads so you can hang the watch on a hook.

The girl on page 43 is showing off the belt and bracelet she made herself. She mounted the knotting strands of the bracelet on a clasp which she purchased at a hobby store. When she had made the bracelet as long as she wanted it, she finished it off by making double knots with the knotting strands around the other end of the clasp. Then she turned the ends of the strands back through the beads and glued them there, and clipped off the excess string.

Illus. 44. A belt or bracelet made from beads plus macramé adds a sporty flair to a simple costume. For a fancier ornament, use shiny cord and crystal beads.

The belt is composed mainly of Diagonal and Horizontal DK bars. The girl mounted six cords on a Fnd. KB of cord, so she had 12 strands for knotting. To make the clasp of the belt, she threaded several beads on the ends of the Fnd. KB and looped the ends to make a round clump of beads. She sewed the ends of the cords in place. If you have a needle with a large enough eye, you could thread the cord through the needle and run it on the underside of the belt through a few knots. A crochet hook can sometimes pull the cord through also.

Since there are beaded "buttons" at one end of the belt, there must be corresponding loops at the other end, to slip the beads through. When the belt is the proper length, finish off the four outer strands on each side of the belt by threading a needle with the cord and drawing it through a few knots. With the remaining four strands, make two SK sennits, long enough to circle the beaded buttons. Turn the sennits to the sides of the belt and fasten the ends in one of the ways described here.

A frame for a picture or mirror, shown closely

Illus. 45. A frame for a round picture or mirror is tricky to make, but can help redecorate a room with little expense. Remember to pull one side tighter than the other, to allow for the curved shape.

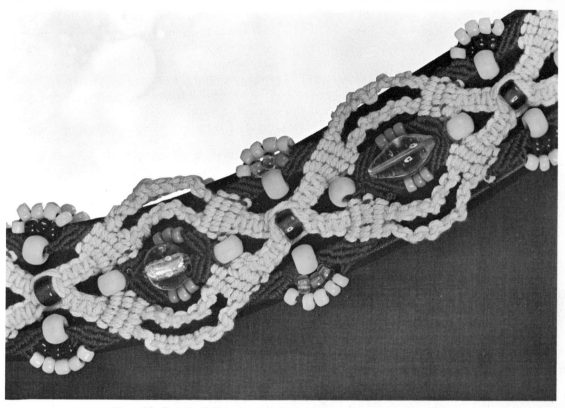

Illus. 46. Detail of the curved picture frame, shown in Illus. 45.

in Illus. 46, should only be attempted after you have made several simpler macramé articles. Because this piece is curved, not straight, the knots on one side must be tighter than those on the other, and less cord allotted for that side. Try making a small piece first so you can gauge how tightly to make the inside knots. The frame here uses two types of yarn: thin carpet yarn (the darker color) and off-white string. The different thicknesses of yarn require two types of beads with holes of different sizes, resulting in a varied yet pleasing arrangement. A frame like this is doubly glamorous, due to its reflection in the mirror it surrounds.

Handbags are among the most practical knotted things you can make. The one pictured in Illus. 47 begins with 24 cords (making 48 strands) mounted on a wood dowel. Secure flat plastic beads at each

Illus. 47. This handbag, in a light color for the spring, is quite sturdy. Heavy cord and many small knots help make it strong.

end of the dowel so the mounted cords do not slip off. This main portion of the bag is made twice, for each side, with Horizontal DK bars, FK sennits and criss-cross FK knots. To attach the two pieces together, insert one long cord through the sides and bottom of each piece, and mount cords on the strand connecting the two parts of the bag. Make a long band of SK's with these cords, wrapping the outside strands through the cord with which you just joined the two pieces.

To make the straps, mount two cords (four strands) on each wood dowel, hanging in the direction opposite that of the bag itself. Make a long FK sennit with each of the four strands. Attach the band at the other side of the dowel by making a double knot with each cord on the dowel and slip the ends through nearby knots. Sew a lining inside the bag.

The handbag in Illus. 48 is made all in one piece (except the handle) and then stitched up the sides to form a pouch. To close the bag at the top, attach a zipper to the ends of the bag. Because of the looseness of the sennits and Diag. DK bars, you should line this bag so that things placed in it do not slip out.

These are only samples of the myriad of unique possibilities you can create with macramé. Use any type of cord, string or twine, in any color, and decorate your knots with big or little beads. The ornaments you make are sure to be unusual, and you should be proud to give them as gifts or use them yourself.

Illus. 48. Another handbag made of macramé knots and decorated with beads. The basic pattern here is diagonal double knot bars, alternating with flat knot sennits.

Index